HIGHLIGHTS OF ENGLISH CATHEDRALS

PAUL SCOTT

INTRODUCTION

In recent years I have made several trips to England with a special project in mind: the photographing in some detail of all the cathedrals of England. The photographs, together with accompanying text, have appeared in publicly accessible websites under the link:
http://paulscottinfo.ipage.com/england/cathedrals/

Many people who have seen the websites or learnt about the project have asked if I plan to publish the results in book form. I have been reluctant to do this. I have taken more than a hundred photographs of many of the cathedrals, and it has seemed like an impossible task to do justice to any cathedral in a couple of printed pages. However, I have come to believe that perhaps the printed version and the underlying websites might be regarded as complementary, rather than in competition. A reader of the printed version might be encouraged to learn more from the website. And the printed version may well be seen as an attractive addition to the home or office coffee table!

Credits
Front cover photo by the author shows Salisbury Cathedral; back cover photo by the author shows Canterbury Cathedral
The minimal text is factual and heavily dependent on Wikipedia.
Nearly all the photographs here are mine. I gratefully acknowledge the following few exceptions, used with permission.
Bradford Cathedral Title Page: BfdCathedral CC BY-SA 4.0
Middlesbrough Cathedral (all photos): Ian Stubbs – Flickr / Bolckow/ St Mary's Cathedral (old and new) Middlesbrough
Newcastle Cathedral Title Page: Paul Carter Flickr / St Nicholas Cathedral
Peterborough Cathedral West Façade: David Iliff CC BY-SA 3.0
St Paul's Cathedral (most photos): Aidan McRae Thomson – Flickr / amthomson / St Paul's Cathedral
Westminster Abbey (all photos): Aidan McRae Thomson – Flickr / amthomson / Westminster Abbey

About the author …
Paul Scott is a retired mathematics professor from the University of Adelaide, Australia, and a member of St Peter's Anglican Cathedral in Adelaide. His interests have included mathematics education, geometric models, playing in brass bands, photography, construction of websites, churches and cathedrals, volcanoes, light houses, windmills…

Email: mail@paulscott.info
Web: http://paulscott.info
Flickr: https://www.flickr.com/photos/paulscottinfo/

Copyright © 2023. All rights reserved. No portion of this publication may be used, reproduced or transmitted by any means, digital, electronic, mechanical, photocopy or recording without written permission of the publisher, except in the case of brief quotations within critical articles or reviews.

ISBN: 978-0-6457817-0-0 (paperback)
ISBN: 978-0-6457817-1-7 (hardcover)

CATHEDRALS

Aldershot RC	4		66	Newcastle
Arundel RC	6		68	Newcastle RC
Birmingham	8		70	Norwich
Birmingham RC	10		72	Norwich RC
Blackburn	12		74	Nottingham RC
Bradford	14		76	Oxford
Brentwood RC	16		78	Peterborough
Bristol	18		80	Plymouth RC
Canterbury	20		82	Portsmouth
Carlisle	22		84	Portsmouth RC
Chelmsford	24		86	Ripon
Chester	26		88	Rochester
Chichester	28		90	Salford RC
Clifton RC	30		92	Salisbury
Coventry	32		94	Sheffield
Derby	34		96	Sheffield RC
Durham	36		98	Shrewsbury RC
Ely	38		100	Southwark
Exeter	40		102	Southwark RC
Gloucester	42		104	Southwell
Guildford	44		106	St Albans
Hereford	46		108	St Edmundsbury
Lancaster RC	48		110	St Pauls
Leeds RC	50		112	Truro
Leicester	52		114	Wakefield
Lichfield	54		116	Wells
Lincoln	56		118	Westminster Abbey
Liverpool	58		120	Westminster Cathedral
Liverpool RC	60		122	Winchester
Manchester	62		124	Worcester
Middlesbrough RC	64		126	York

Chichester Cathedral spire

ALDERSHOT RC

The Cathedral of St Michael and St George in Aldershot serves as the Roman Catholic Cathedral for the Bishopric of the Forces. It was Anglican up until 1973. The Cathedral contains many memorials and some lovely mosaics.

Above West door : St George slays the dragon

Rood made from parts of 23 aircraft

Lady Chapel

Musical Windows

Bell from H.M.S. 'Invincible'

High Altar with surrounding mosaics

ARUNDEL RC

Organ and rose window

Old door in North wall

West rose window

Saint Philip Howard Chapel

The Cathedral Church of Our Lady and St Philip Howard is a Roman Catholic cathedral in Arundel, West Sussex. Dedicated in 1873 as the Catholic parish church of Arundel, it became a cathedral at the foundation of the Diocese of Arundel and Brighton in 1965.

Frieze on steps to St Wilfred's Chapel

Figures above the West door: at centre Mary and Child, and above, a damaged Christ figure

Crucifixion Chapel

Looking down the central aisle to the sanctuary

East Ascension window

Foyer light

The Cathedral Church of Saint Philip is a Church of England cathedral and the seat of the Bishop of Birmingham. Built as a parish church in the Baroque style by Thomas Archer, it was consecrated in 1715, and became a cathedral in 1905. The Cathedral is famous for its stained glass by Edward Burne-Jones.

Interior looking West

BIRMINGHAM RC

Colourful nave roof

Three manual organ

South transept window

The Metropolitan Cathedral Church and Basilica of Saint Chad is a Catholic cathedral in Birmingham. It was designed by A. W. Pugin and was completed by 1841. It was raised to cathedral status in 1852.

Baptismal font

Medieval pulpit

High altar

Patron Saint, St Chad

BLACKBURN

Lantern

Crown of Thorns

Pulpit angel

Blackburn Cathedral, officially known as the Cathedral Church of Blackburn Saint Mary the Virgin with St Paul, is situated in the heart of Blackburn town centre, in Lancashire. The cathedral site has been home to a church for over a thousand years and the first stone church was built there in Norman times. The church obtained cathedral status in 1926.

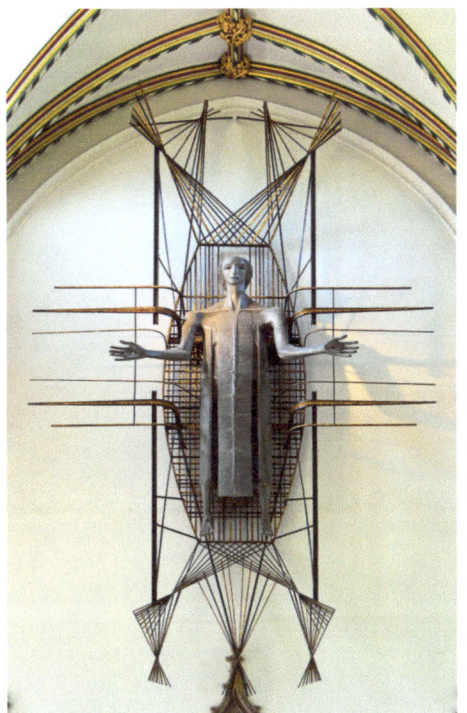

Christ the Worker

Mother and Child

Font figures

Jesus Chapel altar

BRADFORD

Bradford Cathedral Photo

Nave

◀ Cathedral Photo: Wikipedia   ▲ Crests above nave

▲ Sanctuary cross and saints
◀ Cathedra

Bradford Cathedral, called the Cathedral Church of St Peter, is in Bradford, West Yorkshire. It is one of three co-equal cathedrals in the diocese of Leeds alongside Ripon and Wakefield. Its site has been used for Christian worship since the 7th century, when missionaries based in Dewsbury evangelised the area. It achieved cathedral status in 1919.

Mysterious blind staircase

BRENTWOOD RC

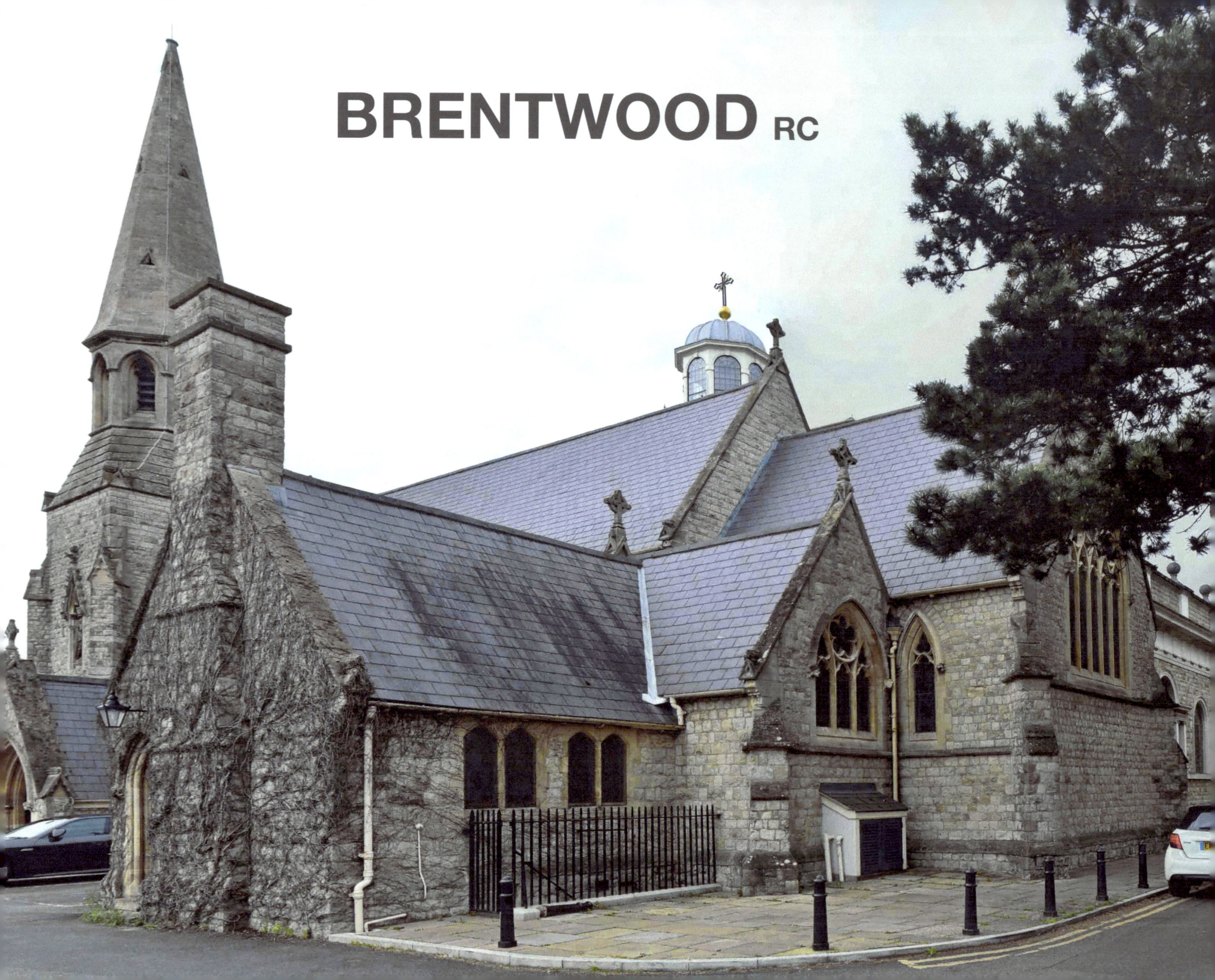

Baptismal font

Processional cross

Corner graves

Brentwood Cathedral, or the Cathedral of St Mary and St Helen, is a Roman Catholic cathedral in Brentwood, Essex. It is the seat of the Diocese of Brentwood. It began in 1861 as a parish church built in a Gothic style and was raised to cathedral status in 1917. Between 1989 and 1991 the church was enlarged in an Italianate classical style by architect Quinlan Terry. The original church building on the East side was retained.

Choir vestry window

Nave

Colourful rear door

Mosaic paving near the High Altar

Cross above the North doors ▶

Bristol Cathedral (the Cathedral Church of the Holy and Undivided Trinity) was founded in 1140 and consecrated in 1148. It was originally St Augustine's Abbey but after the Dissolution of the Monasteries, in 1542 it became the seat of the newly created Bishop of Bristol. It shows a range of building styles, although much of the church was rebuilt in the English Decorated Gothic style in the 14th century. Its peal of eight bells taken from the ruins of Temple Church after the bombing of WWII.

South choir aisle Pentecost window

West rose window

Angel with candlestick

Nautical kneelers

CANTERBURY

Trinity Chapel windows

Font canopy

Beckett memorial

Nave

Canterbury Cathedral, Canterbury, Kent, is one of the oldest and most famous Christian structures in England. It is the cathedral of the Archbishop of Canterbury, leader of the Church of England, and symbolic leader of the world Anglican Communion. Its formal title is the Cathedral and Metropolitan Church of Christ at Canterbury.

Man of Nails in the crypt

CARLISLE

Nave shortened by plundering Scots!

The Border Regiment

Carlisle Cathedral is an Anglican cathedral in the city of Carlisle, Cumbria. It was founded as an Augustinian priory and became a cathedral in 1133. It is also the seat of the Bishop of Carlisle. Carlisle is the second smallest of England's ancient cathedrals.

Painted panel

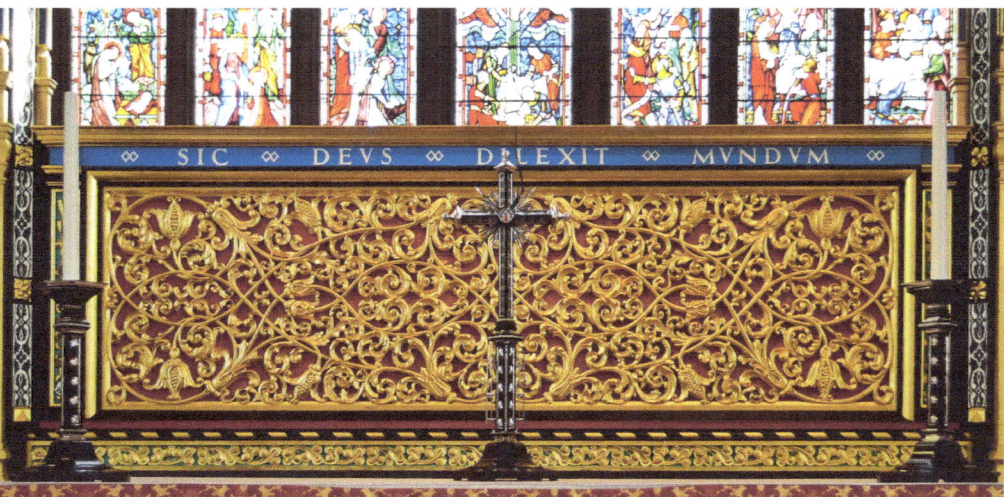
Reredos

Blue barrel roof

CHELMSFORD

Chelmsford Cathedral in the city of Chelmsford, Essex is dedicated to St Mary the Virgin, St Peter and St Cedd. The original church was probably first built along with the town around 1200. It became a cathedral when the Anglican Diocese of Chelmsford was created in 1914. The church has a ring of 13 bells.

Chancel clerestory windows

Holderness window

South porch

'The Ascended Christ' mandorla

Honours Roll and 'rifles'.

'The Tree of Life' painting

Cathedral banner

CHESTER

Chester Cathedral is a Church of England cathedral and the mother church of the Diocese of Chester. The cathedral, formerly the abbey church of a Benedictine monastery dedicated to St Werburgh, is dedicated to Christ and the Blessed Virgin Mary. The cathedral's construction dates from the 10th century, having been modified a number of times throughout history, a typical characteristic of English cathedrals. Since 1541, it has been the seat of the Bishop of Chester.

Left: Nave windows … Above: Nave mosaics

Cloister fountain

St George and the dragon

Nave vaulting

Organ

West rectory window

Choir vaulting

CHICHESTER

Nave

South transept Kings wall painting

St John the Baptist chapel window

Organ

Insignia on Cathedra

High altar and reredos

The Anglican Chichester Cathedral is formally known as the Cathedral Church of the Holy Trinity. It is located in Chichester, in West Sussex. It was founded as a cathedral in 1075. It has fine architecture in both Norman and Gothic styles.

CLIFTON RC

The Cathedral Church of SS. Peter and Paul is the Roman Catholic Cathedral of Clifton, Bristol. It is the seat and mother church of the Diocese of Clifton and is known as Clifton Cathedral. It was the first Cathedral built under new guidelines arising from the Second Vatican Council. Construction began in March 1970 and the building was completed in May 1973. A copper time capsule is placed beneath the foundation stone.

Nave ▶

Ambo and Cathedra

Jubilation windows

Concrete Stations of the Cross, VII – X

In the Lady Chapel

COVENTRY

The Anglican Cathedral Church of Saint Michael, commonly known as Coventry Cathedral, is the seat of the Bishop of Coventry in the West Midlands. The old 14th century St Michael's Church / Cathedral standing adjacent to the present Cathedral remains a ruined shell after its bombing during WWII. The ruined cathedral is a symbol of war time destruction and barbarity, but the present cathedral has a real focus on peace and reconciliation. The words 'Father Forgive' are used as the response in the Coventry Litany of Reconciliation which is prayed in the new Cathedral every weekday at noon.

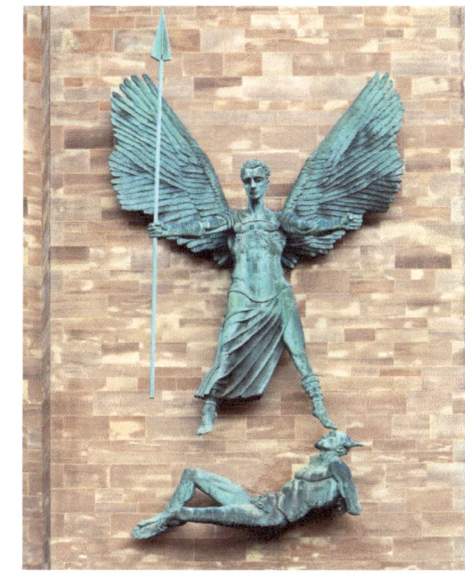

Reconciliation

St Michael's Victory over the Devil

Baptism window   Tapestry of Christ in Glory   North nave windows   ▼ Kneelers   ▲ Chapel of Christ in Gethsemane

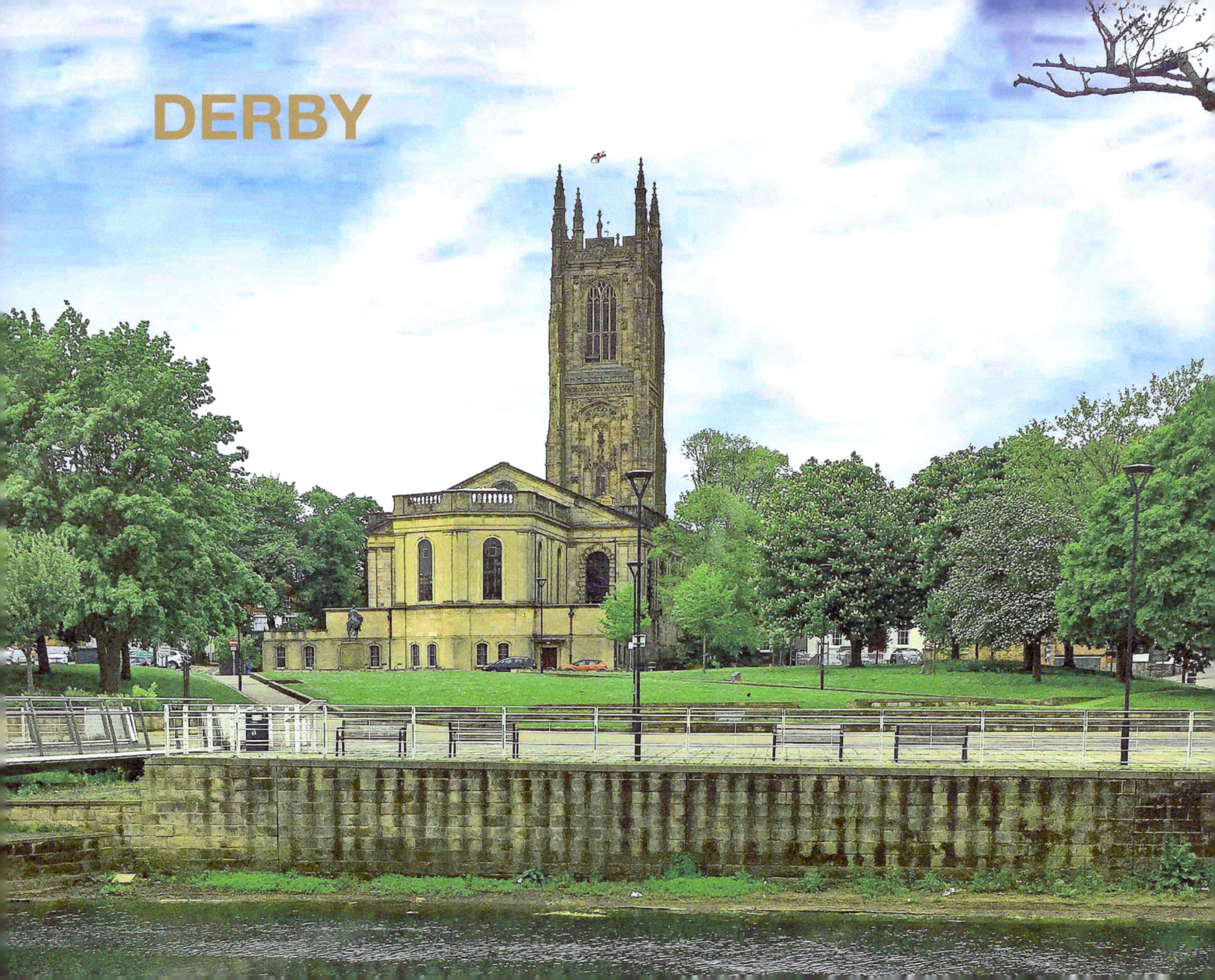

The Cathedral Church of All Saints, Derby, better known as Derby Cathedral, is a cathedral church in the city of Derby. In 1927 it was promoted from parish church to a cathedral, creating a seat for the new Bishop of Derby. The original All Saints church was founded in the mid-10th century as a royal collegiate church. The main body of the church as it stands today is a Georgian rebuilding by James Gibbs, completed in 1725. The tower dates from the 16th century, and a retroquire was added in the 20th century.

Retrochoir organ

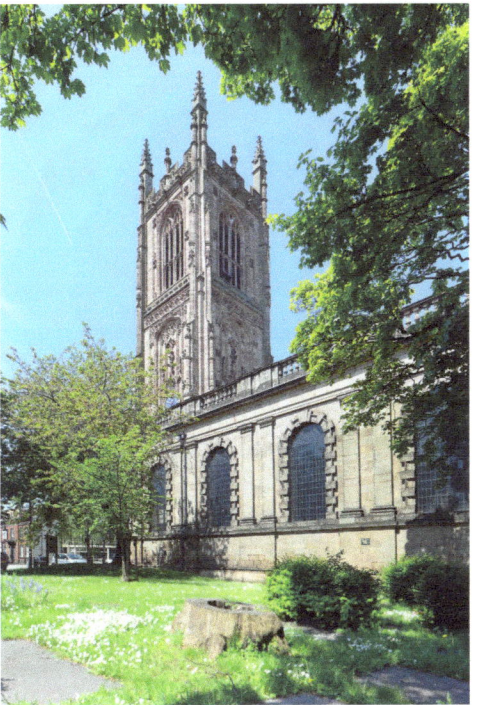
Tower and South wall

Dramatic wrought iron screens

Organ

The 'mixed and massive piles' (Sir Walter Scott)

The sanctuary knocker

King Oswald window in the nave

Durham Cathedral is the Cathedral Church of Christ, Blessed Mary the Virgin and St Cuthbert of Durham, and is home of the Shrine of St Cuthbert. It is a cathedral in the city of Durham, County Durham in the north of England. It is the seat of the Bishop of Durham, the fourth-ranked bishop in the Church of England hierarchy. Building of the present Norman era cathedral started in 1093. The Cathedral has a complicated history, with the See of Durham taking its origins from the Diocese of Lindisfarne founded by Saint Aidan at the behest of Oswald of Northumbria in about 635.

Tomb of Venerable Bede, Galilee Chapel

Chapter house windows

Shrine of St Cuthbert

Colourful nave ceiling

Ely Cathedral, or the Cathedral Church of the Holy and Undivided Trinity, is an Anglican cathedral in the city of Ely, Cambridgeshire. The cathedral has its origins in AD 672 when St Etheldreda built an abbey church. The present building dates back to 1083, and it was granted cathedral status in 1109. Until the Reformation it was the Church of St Etheldreda and St Peter, at which point it was refounded as the Cathedral Church of the Holy and Undivided Trinity of Ely.

The famous 'Ely lantern'

Wonderful narthex symbolism

Virgin Mary in the Lady Chapel

Choir screen arch

Lantern figures (opening doors)

EXETER

Exeter Cathedral, properly known as the Cathedral Church of Saint Peter in Exeter, is an Anglican cathedral, and the seat of the Bishop of Exeter in the city of Exeter, Devon. The present building was completed by about 1400, and has several notable features, including an early set of misericords, an astronomical clock, the organ, and the longest uninterrupted medieval stone vaulted ceiling in the world.

Minstrel Gallery in nave

Column capitals

Nave

High altar cross

Carved choir figure

Bishop Stafford tomb

Giant boss

GLOUCESTER

Holy Family – Josefina de Vasconcellos

◄West nave   Organ ▲

Gloucester Cathedral, formally the Cathedral Church of St Peter and the Holy and Indivisible Trinity, in Gloucester, stands in the north of the city near the River Severn. It originated with the establishment of a minster dedicated to Saint Peter and founded by Osric, King of the Hwicce, in around 679. The subsequent history of the church is complex. The present building was begun by Abbott Serlo in about 1089, following a major fire the previous year. The church was formerly an abbey which was dissolved in 1540, and then became a cathedral in 1541.

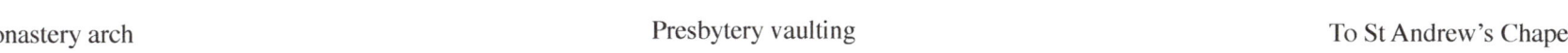

Monastery arch   Presbytery vaulting   To St Andrew's Chapel

GUILDFORD

Sanctuary round window

Regimental chapel altar

Baptistry

North Aisle ▲
High Altar cross ▶
Treasury items ▼

The Cathedral Church of the Holy Spirit, Guildford, usually known as Guildford Cathedral, is the Anglican cathedral at Guildford, Surrey. Land was given by Richard Onslow and Viscount Bennett. The Cathedral was designed by Edward Maufe and built between 1936 and 1961. It is the seat of the Bishop of Guildford. More than 200,000 people bought a brick for the building of the Cathedral.

Chained Library

Hereford Cathedral is the Cathedral Church of the Anglican Diocese of Hereford in Hereford. A place of worship has existed on the site of the present building since the 8th century or earlier. The present building was begun in 1079. Substantial parts of the building date from both the Norman and the Gothic periods. The Cathedral has the largest library of chained books in the world, its most famous treasure being the Mappa Mundi, a medieval map of the world created around 1300 by Richard of Holdingham. The Cathedral is dedicated to two saints, St Mary the Virgin and St Ethelbert the King.

Choir angel

Misericord

Shrine of Thomas

Nave

North transept window

LANCASTER RC

View from canal

Nave

Lancaster Cathedral (The Cathedral Church of St Peter, Saint Peter's Cathedral), is a Roman Catholic cathedral in Lancaster, Lancashire. It was a Roman Catholic parish church until 1924, when it was elevated to the status of a cathedral. It is built in Gothic Revival style.

Original High Altar reredos – now in Blessed Sacrament Chapel

Madonna and Child – local artist

Archway to baptistry

Stations of the Cross

LEEDS RC

Garden walk approach

Nave

Lampedusa Cross

Leeds Cathedral, (Cathedral Church of St Anne, or Saint Anne's Cathedral) is the cathedral of the Roman Catholic Diocese of Leeds and is the seat of the Roman Catholic Bishop of Leeds. It is in the city of Leeds, West Yorkshire. The original cathedral was located in nearby St Anne's Church in 1878, but that building was demolished around 1900. The current cathedral building on Cookridge Street was completed in 1904, and was restored in 2006. It was designed in the Arts and Crafts Gothic Revival style by John Henry Eastwood.

Organ pipes

Sanctuary with mosaics

Lady Chapel mosaics

Cathedra (Bishop's throne)

Nave

St Katherine Chapel altar

The Cathedral Church of Saint Martin, Leicester (Leicester Cathedral), is a Church of England cathedral in Leicester. The church was elevated to a collegiate church in 1922 and made a cathedral in 1927 following the establishment of a new Diocese of Leicester. The remains of King Richard III were reburied in the cathedral in 2015 after being discovered nearby.

Tomb of King Richard III

Abraham icon

The West wall

Inside the nave

Screen door, North choir aisle

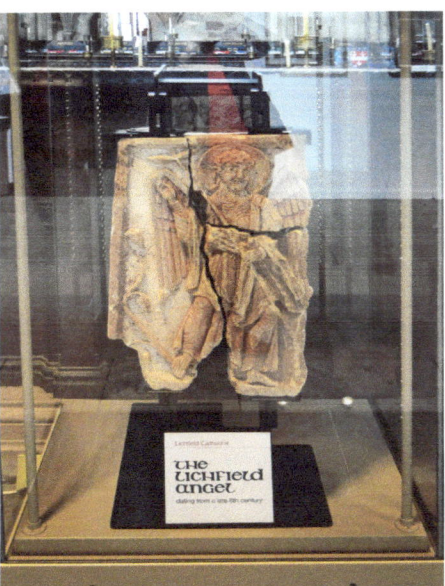

The Lichfield Angel

Lichfield Cathedral is an Anglican cathedral in Lichfield, Staffordshire, one of only three cathedrals in the United Kingdom with three spires (together with Truro Cathedral and St Mary's Cathedral in Edinburgh), and the only medieval one of the three. It is the cathedral of the Diocese of Lichfield, which covers Staffordshire, much of Shropshire, and parts of the Black Country and West Midlands. It is notable for its red sandstone, and 'busy' West wall. The three spires are often referred to as the 'Ladies of the Vale'.

Nave altar 'Tree of Life'

Historic tiling by High Altar

Rummer Goblet, South choir aisle

Chapter house

Frieze: the grisly fate of sinners

Lincoln Cathedral, (Lincoln Minster, or the Cathedral Church of the Blessed Virgin Mary of Lincoln) in Lincoln, is the seat of the Anglican Bishop of Lincoln. Building commenced in 1072 and continued in several phases throughout the High Middle Ages. Like many of the medieval Cathedrals of England, it was built in the Early Gothic style.

Crossing roof

The Bishop's Eye

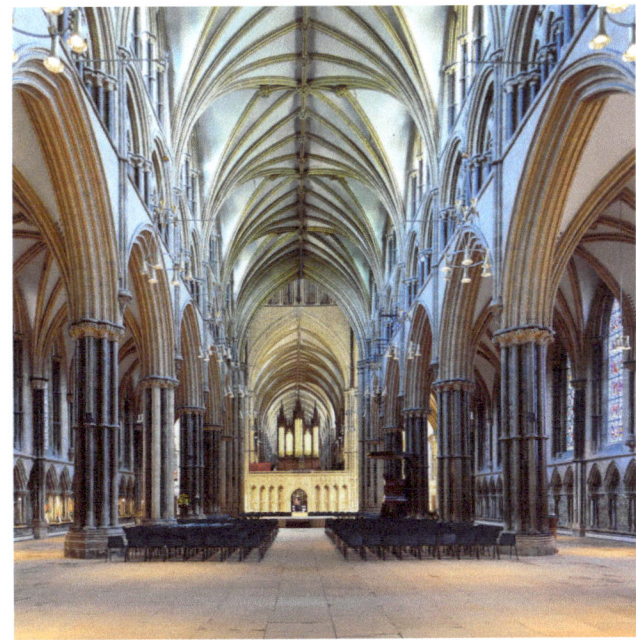
Nave

'Forest Stations': stations of the cross by William Fairbank

West window

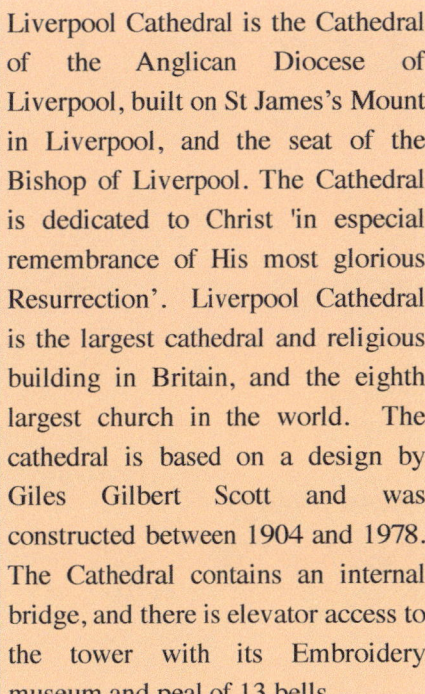
Holy Spirit Chapel

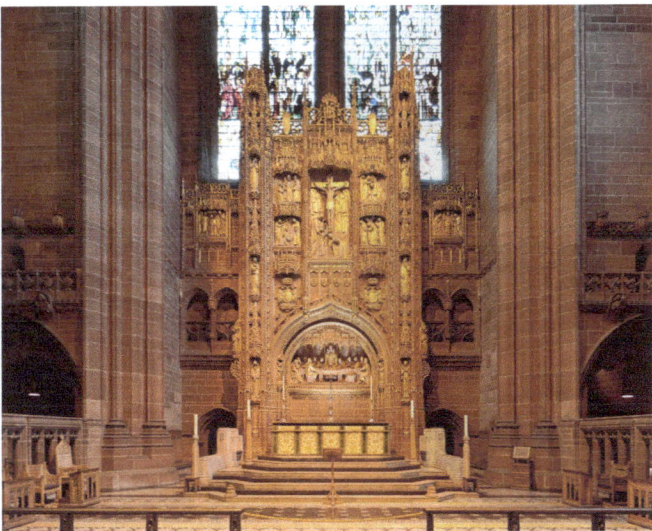
High altar

Nave view from bridge to high altar

Liverpool Cathedral is the Cathedral of the Anglican Diocese of Liverpool, built on St James's Mount in Liverpool, and the seat of the Bishop of Liverpool. The Cathedral is dedicated to Christ 'in especial remembrance of His most glorious Resurrection'. Liverpool Cathedral is the largest cathedral and religious building in Britain, and the eighth largest church in the world. The cathedral is based on a design by Giles Gilbert Scott and was constructed between 1904 and 1978. The Cathedral contains an internal bridge, and there is elevator access to the tower with its Embroidery museum and peal of 13 bells.

Museum of Ecclesiastical Embroidery

LIVERPOOL RC

Circular nave

Central lantern

Children's Chapel

Abraham

Liverpool Metropolitan Cathedral, officially known as the Metropolitan Cathedral of Christ the King and locally nicknamed 'Paddy's Wigwam', is the seat of the Archbishop of Liverpool and the mother church of the Roman Catholic Diocese of Liverpool in Liverpool. The cathedral's architect was Frederick Gibbard. Construction began in 1962 and was completed in 1967. The cathedral has a circular nave surrounded by 13 chapels.

Joseph's workshop

Banner above baptistry entrance

Station XII

Manchester Cathedral, formally the Cathedral and Collegiate Church of St Mary, St Denys and St George, in Manchester, is the mother church of the Anglican Diocese of Manchester, and the city's parish church. The former parish church, rebuilt in the Perpendicular Gothic style in 1421 but since extensively altered, became a cathedral in 1847. The church was badly damaged by a German bomb in 1940.

West window

Regimental Chapel

East window

Organ

Cross in Jesus Chapel

Baptismal font

Figure on reading stand

MIDDLESBROUGH RC

All photos : Ian Stubbs

Saint Mary's Cathedral, also known as Middlesbrough Cathedral, is a Roman Catholic Cathedral in Coulby Newham, Middlesbrough. It is the see of the Bishop of Middlesbrough. The original Cathedral Church of Our Lady Of Perpetual Succour was built from 1876 and was opened in 1878. In 1984, news reports stated that the old cathedral had structural problems and might have to be pulled down. It was gutted by fire in May 2000, and the building was demolished soon after. The new cathedral was consecrated in 1998.

Nave of Old St Mary's

Sanctuary (top) and Blessed Sacrament Chapel

Old Cathedral after the fire　　　　The Holy Family　　　　Sanctuary Cross　　　　Station of the Cross

NEWCASTLE

This photo: Paul Carter

Newcastle Cathedral, (the Cathedral Church of St Nicholas), is a Church of England cathedral in Newcastle upon Tyne. It is the seat of the Bishop of Newcastle. Founded in 1091, the Norman church was destroyed by fire in 1216 and the current building was completed in 1350, so is mostly of the Perpendicular style of the 14th century. The unusual lantern spire was used for navigation for hundreds of years by ships on the River Tyne.

Clock Window in crypt The Venerable Bede Baptismal Font

Madonna and Child Crypt Windows

Exterior fence text: Benedict terra Domino: laudet et superexaltet eum in saecula. (Let the earth bless the Lord; let it praise and exalt Him above all forever.)

NEWCASTLE RC

West nave

Musical angels

The Cathedral Church of St Mary is a Catholic cathedral in Newcastle upon Tyne. It is the mother church of the Diocese of Hexham and Newcastle, and seat of the Bishop of Hexham and Newcastle. The cathedral is situated on Clayton Street, was designed by Augustus Welby Pugin and was built between 1842 and 1844. The cathedral is a fine example of the Gothic Revival style of architecture championed by Pugin. It contains a three-manual Kenneth Tickell organ of 46 stops.

South nave window

Baptismal font

Cathedra

High altar

NORWICH

West window

Organ

St Saviour's Chapel

Stag on choir screen

Norwich Cathedral is an Anglican cathedral in Norwich, Norfolk, dedicated to the Holy and Undivided Trinity. It is the cathedral church for the Diocese of Norfolk. The cathedral was begun in 1096 and constructed out of flint and mortar and faced with a cream-coloured Caen limestone. The cathedral was completed in 1145 with the Norman tower still seen today topped with a wooden spire covered with lead.

Altar mosaic

South transept clock: Gog and Magog

Unusual pelican lectern

NORWICH RC

Nave

The Cathedral Church of St John the Baptist is the Roman Catholic Cathedral of the city of Norwich, Norfolk. The cathedral was constructed between 1882 and 1910 to designs by George Gilbert Scott Jr as a parish church dedicated to John the Baptist, on the site of the Norwich City Gaol. The funds for its construction were provided by Henry Fitzalan-Howard, 15th Duke of Norfolk as a gesture of thanksgiving for his first marriage to Lady Flora Abney-Hastings. In 1976, it was consecrated as the cathedral church for the newly erected Diocese of East Anglia and the seat of the Bishop of East Anglia.

St Anthony

Madonna and Child

Interior West doors

Nave column cross

The Annunciation

Nave grisaille window

NOTTINGHAM RC

Nave

Blessed Sacrament Chapel

Eastern walls

Cathedra

The Cathedral Church of St. Barnabas is a cathedral of the Roman Catholic Church in the city of Nottingham in Nottinghamshire. It is the mother church of the Diocese of Nottingham and seat of the Bishop of Nottingham. It was built between 1841 and 1844, and was first consecrated in 1844, fifteen years after the Catholic Relief Act ended most restrictions on Catholicism in the United Kingdom. The architect was Augustus Welby Pugin. It was built in the Early English Plain Gothic style, although in contrast, the Blessed Sacrament Chapel was richly decorated and Pugin's later churches were built in that Decorated Gothic style.

West Window

OXFORD

Christ Church Cathedral is the cathedral of the Anglican Diocese of Oxford, which is made up of the three counties of Oxfordshire, Buckinghamshire, and Berkshire. It is also the chapel of Christ Church, a college of the University of Oxford. This dual role as cathedral and college chapel is unique in the Church of England. The cathedral was originally the church of St Frideswide's Priory. The site was historically presumed to be the location of the nunnery founded by St Frideswide, the patron saint of Oxford, and the shrine is now in the Latin Chapel.

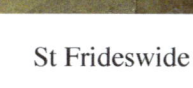

High altar — North aisle window — St Frideswide

Choir stalls carving — Choir stalls — Vaulting

Nave

Old clock

West wall [Photo Credit: David Iliff]

Peterborough Cathedral (Cathedral Church of St Peter, St Paul and St Andrew) is the seat of the Anglican Bishop of Peterborough, dedicated to Saint Peter, Saint Paul and Saint Andrew, whose statues look down from the three high gables of the famous West Front. Although it was founded in the Anglo-Saxon period, its architecture is mainly Norman, following a rebuilding in the 12th century. With Durham and Ely cathedrals, it is one of the most important 12th-century buildings in England to have remained largely intact.

Nave roof

Nave altar

Lady of Lamentation

Apse roof

PLYMOUTH RC

Entrance

West nave

Corona

Paschal candle

The Cathedral Church of Saint Mary and Saint Boniface, Plymouth, is mother church of the Roman Catholic Diocese of Plymouth, covering Cornwall, Devon and Dorset. The Diocese of Plymouth was created in 1850. The cathedral is also used by Royal Navy personnel stationed at HMNB Devonport for the annual naval mass.

Stations of the Cross

High altar

PORTSMOUTH

▼ Golden Barque   ▲ Garden entry   Nave   'Mary Rose'   ▲ Cathedral emblem   ▼ Pyx

The Cathedral Church of St Thomas of Canterbury, Portsmouth Cathedral, is an Anglican cathedral church in the centre of Old Portsmouth. It is the cathedral of the Diocese of Portsmouth. Around the year 1180, Jean de Gisors, a wealthy Norman merchant and Lord of the Manor of Titchfield, gave land in his new town of Portsmouth to the Augustinian canons of Southwick Priory. It was given so that they could build a chapel dedicated to the honour of Sir Thomas of Canterbury, who was assassinated and martyred ten years earlier. The medieval building, dedicated in 1188, was cruciform in shape, with a central tower which was used as a lookout point and lighthouse. This chapel was to become, in turn, a parish church in the 14th century and then a cathedral in the 20th century.

Quire windows

83

PORTSMOUTH RC

Rood cross

Nave

Nave vaulting

St Patrick

The Cathedral Church of St John the Evangelist (St John's Cathedral) is a Roman Catholic cathedral in Portsmouth. The cathedral was designed in Gothic Revival style by John Crawley in 1877–1881 and dedicated in 1882. It is built of Fareham red brick with Portland stone dressings. A bronze statue of St John the Evangelist, by sculptor Philip Jackson, stands eight feet tall outside the cathedral. The Bishop's House next door to the cathedral was destroyed by a bomb in 1941. While the main structure of the cathedral itself was mostly unharmed, all the stained glass, except for the rose window in the South transept was damaged or destroyed.

Famous people in the Lady Chapel

Last Supper window

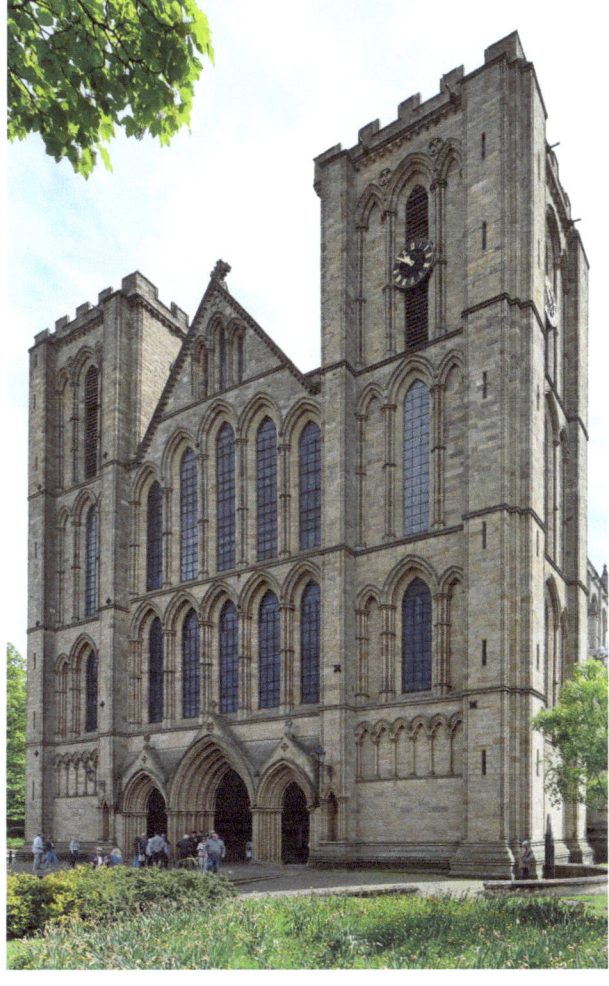

The Cathedral Church of St Peter and St Wilfrid (Ripon Cathedral), is a cathedral in Ripon, North Yorkshire. Founded as a monastery by monks of the Irish tradition in the 660s, it was refounded as a Benedictine monastery by St Wilfrid in 672. The present church is the fourth, and was built between the 13th and 16th centuries. In 1836 the church became the cathedral for the Diocese of Ripon.

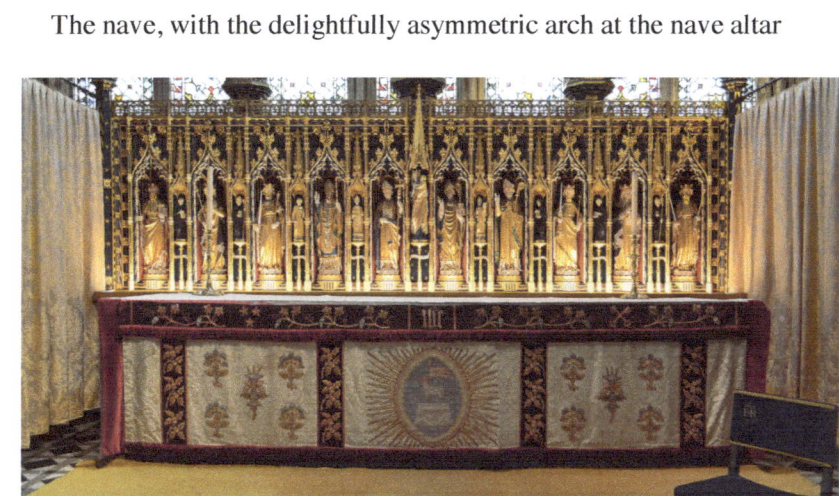

The nave, with the delightfully asymmetric arch at the nave altar

West wall   To choir and sanctuary   High altar

Pulpitum figures

ROCHESTER

Crossing

Rochester Cathedral, formally the Cathedral Church of Christ and the Blessed Virgin Mary, is an English church of Norman architecture in Rochester, Kent. The church is the cathedral of the Diocese of Rochester in the Church of England and the seat (cathedra) of the Bishop of Rochester, the second oldest bishopric in England after that of the Archbishop of Canterbury. Its cathedral status dates from 604, with founder St Justus, who was one of the missionaries who accompanied Augustine of Canterbury to convert the pagan southern English to Christianity in the early 7th century.

West door

Cathedra coats of arms

Baptismal font

Madonna

Choir stall ends

Nave

The Cathedral Church of St. John the Evangelist (Salford Cathedral), is a Catholic cathedral on Chapel Street in Salford, Greater Manchester. It is the seat of the Bishop of Salford. It was built between 1844 and 1848 to designs of Matthew Ellison Hadfield of Sheffield. The 1994 abstract window is said to show the crucified Christ With the Virgin Mary and St John.

Sacred Heart Chapel mosaic

Painting of Joseph

West window

War Memorial Chapel

Nave and font

Trinity Chapel

St Michael

Geometric cloister

Salisbury Cathedral, (the Cathedral Church of the Blessed Virgin Mary), is an Anglican cathedral in Salisbury. The cathedral is the mother church of the Diocese of Salisbury and is the seat of the Bishop of Salisbury. The building is regarded as one of the leading examples of Early English Gothic architecture. Its main body was completed in 38 years, from 1220 to 1258. The spire, built in 1320, at 404 feet (123 m), has been the tallest church spire in the United Kingdom since 1561. The cathedral has the largest cloister in Britain.

Audrey Chapel vaulting

Inside the spire

SHEFFIELD

Nave

Sanctuary angels

West Lantern

West window

Sheffield Cathedral, The Cathedral Church of St Peter and St Paul, Sheffield, is the cathedral church for the Church of England Sheffield, England. Originally a parish church, it was elevated to cathedral status when the diocese was created in 1914. Construction of the earliest section of the cathedral dates back to c. 1200, with the newest construction completed in 1966; the building is an unusual mixture of medieval and modern architecture. Most recently, the cathedral underwent an interior and exterior refurbishment in 2013–2014.

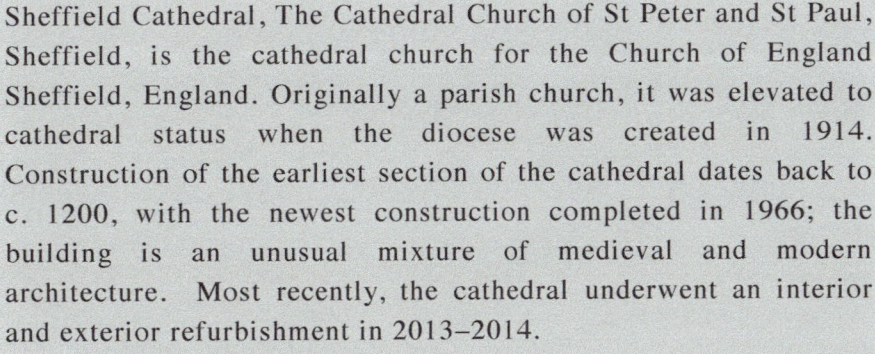

Altar figures

Steel Nativity

SHEFFIELD RC

Chapel dome

Decorated capital

High altar

The Cathedral Church of St Marie is the Roman Catholic cathedral in Sheffield. It lies in a slightly hidden location, just off Fargate shopping street, but signals its presence with a tall spire. It is an especially fine example of an English Roman Catholic Cathedral, with much fine interior decoration. Re-ordering of the sanctuary following the Second Vatican Council, has been sensitive. There are several particularly notable side altars, as well as historic statues and painted tiles.

Nave

Sanctuary roof

Rood cross

Great East window

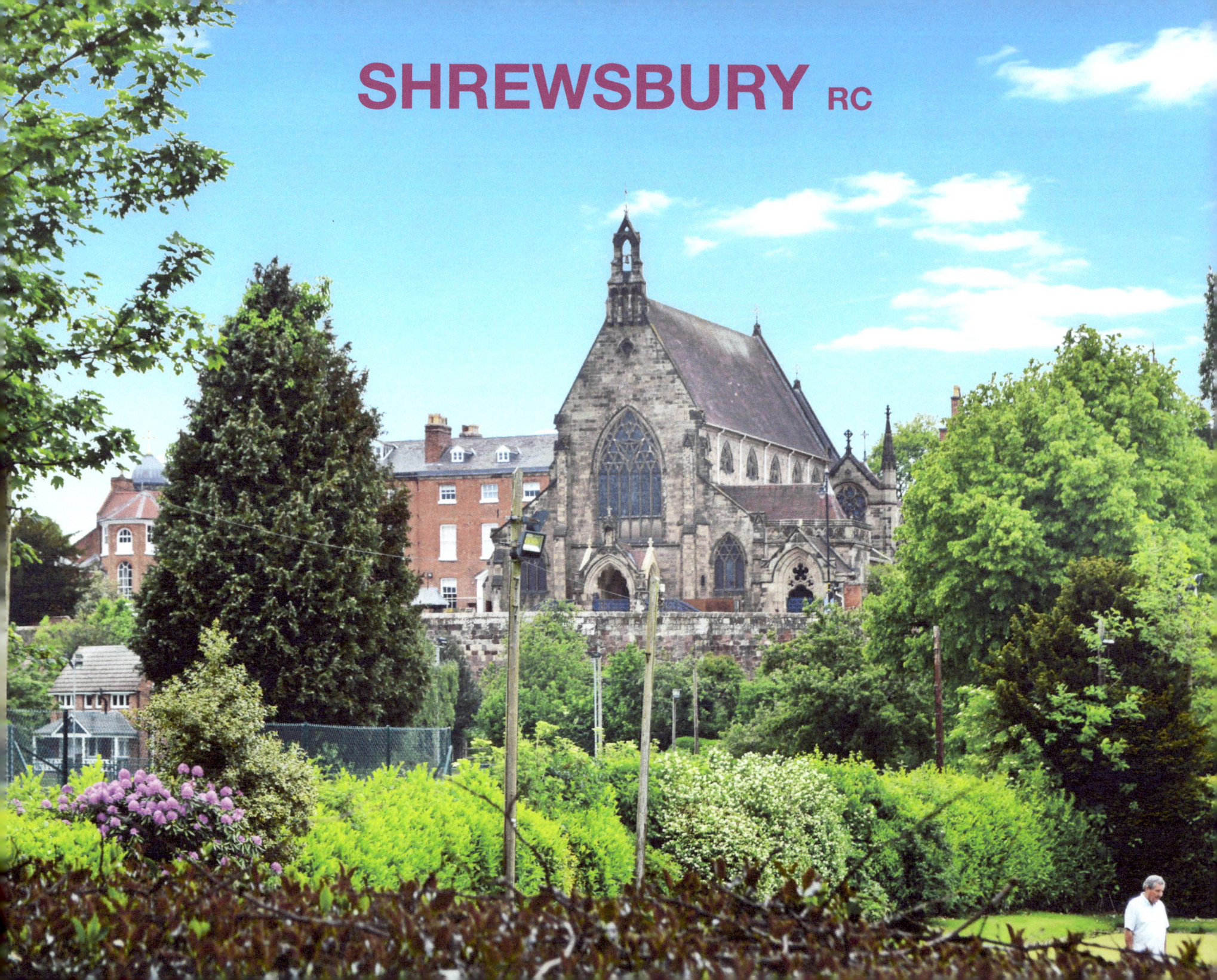

West wall

St Winefride

Rood Cross

Nave looking West

The Cathedral Church of Our Lady Help of Christians and Saint Peter of Alcantara, or Shrewsbury Cathedral, is a Roman Catholic Cathedral in Shrewsbury. It is the seat of the Roman Catholic Bishop of Shrewsbury and mother church of the Diocese of Shrewsbury which covers the historic counties of Shropshire and Cheshire. The cathedral is notable as being the only cathedral in the county.

St Joseph

St Winefride Chapel

Sanctuary lamp

High altar

SOUTHWARK

Short history

Virgin and Child on the high altar

Harvard Chapel painting

In memory of John Harvard

Southwark Cathedral, or The Cathedral and Collegiate Church of St Saviour and St Mary Overie, Southwark, lies on the south bank of the River Thames. It is the mother church of the Anglican Diocese of Southwark. It has been a place of Christian worship for more than 1,000 years, but a cathedral only since 1905.

Baptismal font

Nave

Font canopy

Colourful crossing roof

SOUTHWARK RC

Nave

Petre Chantry altar

The Metropolitan Cathedral Church of St George, or St George's Cathedral, Southwark, is the cathedral of the Roman Catholic Archdiocese in Southwark, South London, and is the seat of the Archbishop of Southwark. The building was erected in 1848 and reopened in 1958 after extensive war damage was repaired.

West window

Divine Child statue

Romero Cross

St Joseph

Chancel roof

Pilgrims' Chapel cross

Southwell Minster is a minster and cathedral in Southwell, Nottinghamshire. It is situated 6 miles (9.7 km) from Newark-on-Trent and 13 miles (21 km) from Mansfield. It is the seat of the Bishop of Southwell and Nottingham and the Diocese of Southwell and Nottingham. The history of the site dates from 627, but the minster became a cathedral in 1884. The recommended pronunciation of the name is 'Suth-ell', but the 'South-well' alternative is also used.

Pulpit detail

Grisaille windows

Nave with Norman columns

Pilgrims' Chapel painting

(Top and bottom) The unique 14 Stations of the Cross

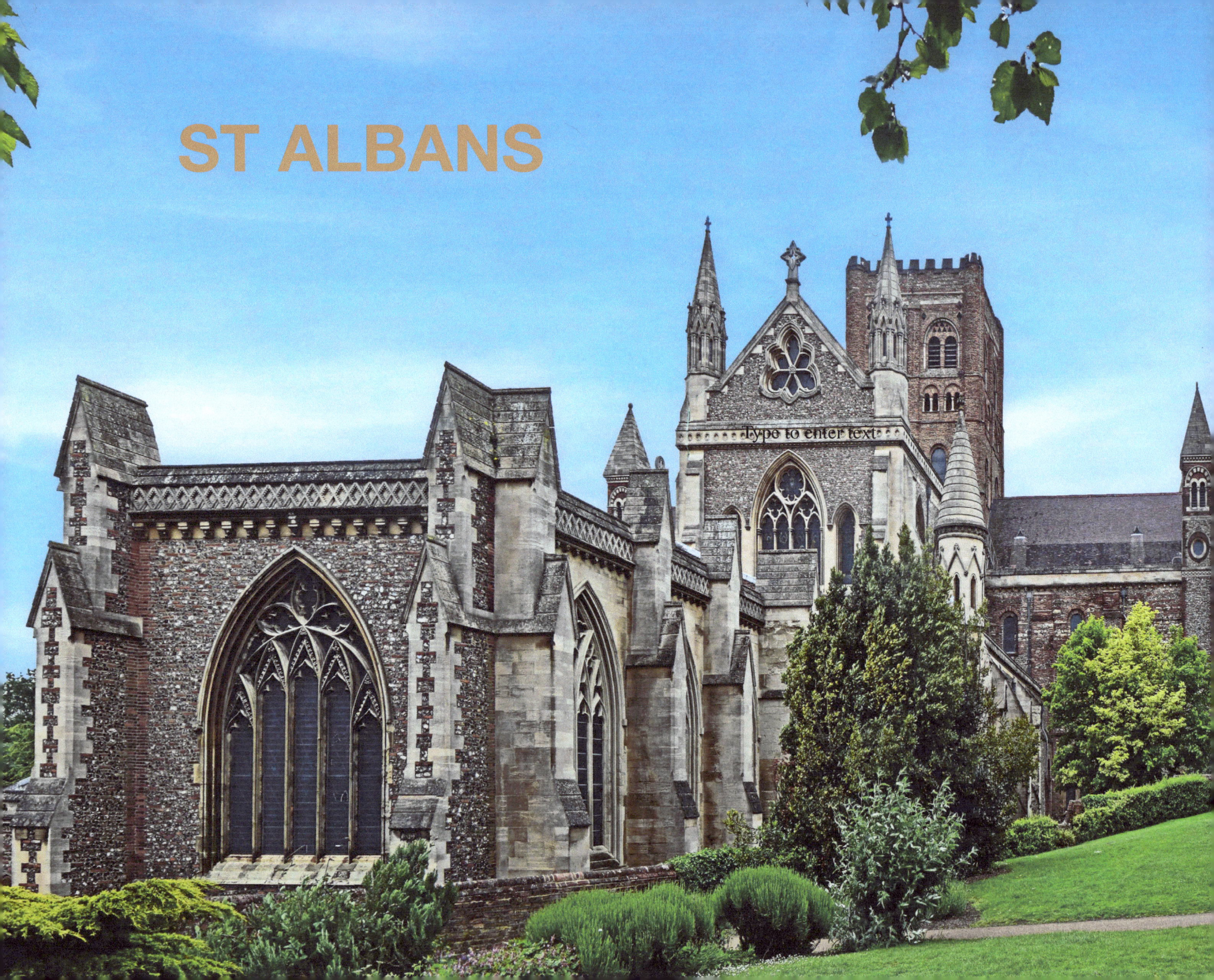
ST ALBANS

Wall painting

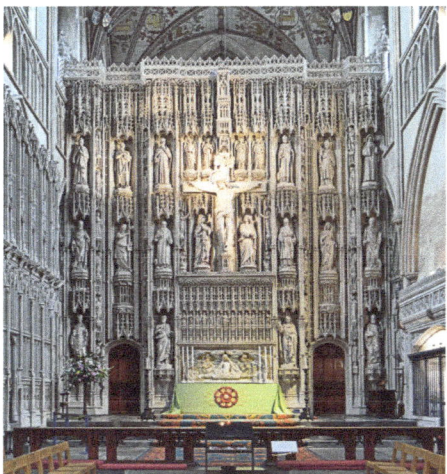
Main altar reredos

North transept window

Nave reredos: seven martyrs

Crossing roof

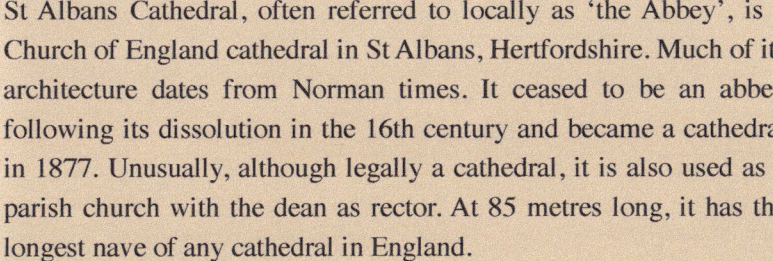

St Albans Cathedral, often referred to locally as 'the Abbey', is a Church of England cathedral in St Albans, Hertfordshire. Much of its architecture dates from Norman times. It ceased to be an abbey following its dissolution in the 16th century and became a cathedral in 1877. Unusually, although legally a cathedral, it is also used as a parish church with the dean as rector. At 85 metres long, it has the longest nave of any cathedral in England.

History panorama

ST EDMUNDSBURY

Death of St Edmund

Madonna and Child

Nave looking West

The Wolf and the Head

St Edmundsbury Cathedral (The Cathedral Church of St James and St Edmund) is the cathedral for the Church of England's Diocese of St Edmundsbury and Ipswich. It is in Bury St Edmunds in Suffolk. Originating in the 11th century, it was rebuilt in the 12th century, and again in the 16th century in the Perpendicular Style as a Parish church. It became a cathedral in 1914. It has been considerably enlarged from 1959 onwards with the addition of transepts, a Lady Chapel, and a side chapel dedicated to St Edmund.

Pipe organ

Transept roof

ST PAUL'S

All the small photos are by Aidan McRae Thomson

Nave

OBE Chapel in the crypt

Looking up to the dome

St Paul's Cathedral is an Anglican Cathedral in London, and is the seat of the Bishop of London. The cathedral serves as the mother church of the Diocese of London. It is on Ludgate Hill, at the highest point of the City of London. Its dedication to Paul the Apostle dates back to the original church on this site, founded in AD 604. The present structure, dating from the late 17th century, was designed in the English Baroque style by Sir Christopher Wren. Its construction, completed in Wren's lifetime, was part of a major rebuilding programme in the city after the Great Fire of London.

Tijou Gate in the sanctuary

'Light of the World'

Great War Sculpture

Lord Nelson tomb

The Cathedral of the Blessed Virgin Mary is a Church of England cathedral in the city of Truro, Cornwall. It was built between 1880 and 1910 to a Gothic Revival design by John Loughborough Pearson on the site of the parish church of St Mary. It is one of only three cathedrals in the United Kingdom featuring three spires. It is also interesting in that in order for the nave to be built, there is a deliberate noticeable 'kink' at the crossing.

West rose window

Main altar reredos: bottom angels at top left

Top: reredos angels; Above: nave; Below: carved panel in quire

Cathedra

Wesley window

WAKEFIELD

Font

Prayer tree

Bright, light nave

Wakefield Cathedral, or the Cathedral Church of All Saints in Wakefield, West Yorkshire, is a co-equal Anglican cathedral with Bradford and Ripon Cathedrals, in the Diocese of Leeds. Originally the parish church, it has Anglo Saxon origins and, after enlargement and rebuilding, has the tallest spire in Yorkshire. Its 247-foot (75 m) spire is the tallest structure in the City of Wakefield. The church became a cathedral in 1888. It has responsibility for the little chantry chapel on Wakefield Bridge, a short distance away.

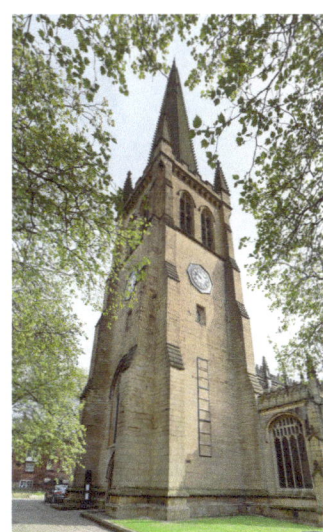

Tower

Candelabra

Detail of main reredos

Cross sculpture in the Garden

Famous scissor arch

Wells Cathedral is an Anglican cathedral in Wells, Somerset, dedicated to St Andrew the Apostle. It is the seat of the Bishop of Bath and of Wells whose cathedra it holds. Built as a Roman Catholic cathedral from around 1175 to replace an earlier church on the site since 705, it became an Anglican cathedral when King Henry VIII split from Rome. It is moderately sized for an English cathedral. It has been called 'unquestionably one of the most beautiful' and 'most poetic' of English cathedrals. Its Gothic architecture is mostly inspired from the Early English style of the late 12th to early 13th centuries. In the 14th century the famous scissor arches were inserted to stabilise the piers supporting the central tower.

Vicars' Close

Vaulting of Lady Chapel

Altar piece in St Martin's Chapel

Stations of the Cross

WESTMINSTER ABBEY

This page: Photo credit: CC Wikipedia giggel
All small photo credits: Aidan McRae Thomson

Superb vaulting of Lady Chapel

Nave altar and choir screen

Nave window

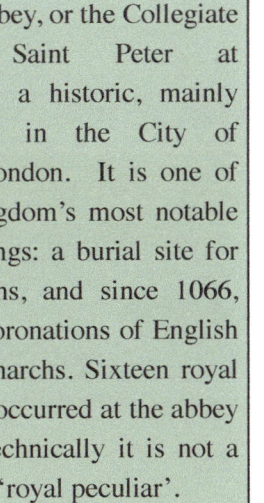
West face

Westminster Abbey, or the Collegiate Church of Saint Peter at Westminster, is a historic, mainly Gothic church in the City of Westminster, London. It is one of the United Kingdom's most notable religious buildings: a burial site for British monarchs, and since 1066, the site of all coronations of English and British monarchs. Sixteen royal weddings have occurred at the abbey since 1100. Technically it is not a cathedral, but a 'royal peculiar'.

Monck monument

Crossing roof

Triforium view

Lady Chapel

Pope St Gregory the Great

Station of the cross VIII

Cathedral tower

Westminster Cathedral is the mother church of the Catholic Church in England and Wales. It is the largest Catholic church in the UK. The site on which the cathedral stands in the City of Westminster (London) was purchased in 1885, and construction was completed in 1903. It was designed by John Francis Bentley in neo-Byzantine style, and accordingly made almost entirely of brick, without steel reinforcements. It is often overlooked by visitors to London, which is a great pity.

Chapel of St George and the English Martyrs

St Peter

WINCHESTER

Nave

Diver memorial

Elegant choir pulpit

Joan of Arc

Crossing roof

West face

The Cathedral Church of the Holy Trinity, St Peter, St Paul and St Swithun, known as Winchester Cathedral, is the cathedral of the city of Winchester, and is the longest medieval cathedral in the world. Its cathedral status dates from 662, but the present building dates from 1079 – 1532. The architectural style is Norman with Gothic extensions. Around 1900 the Cathedral had been in danger of collapse as it sank into the ground. The situation was remedied by diver William Walker who between 1906 and 1911 shored up the foundations.

Retrochoir icons above the St Swithun's hole

Nave vaulting

WORCESTER

Cloisters

Baptismal Font

Misericords

Worcester Cathedral is an Anglican cathedral in Worcester, in Worcestershire, situated on a bank overlooking the River Severn. It is the seat of the Bishop of Worcester. Its official name is the Cathedral Church of Christ and the Blessed Mary the Virgin, of Worcester. The present cathedral church was built between 1084 and 1504, and represents every style of English architecture from Norman to Perpendicular Gothic. The cathedral contains the tombs of King John and Prince Arthur.

West face

Pipe organ

High altar

Constantine the Great

Decorated Cross in crypt

Headless semaphore figures: 'Christ is Here'

The Cathedral and Metropolitical Church of Saint Peter in York, commonly known as York Minster, is the cathedral of York, North Yorkshire, and is one of the largest of its kind in Northern Europe. The minster is the seat of the Archbishop of York, the third-highest office of the Church of England (after the monarch as Supreme Governor and the Archbishop of Canterbury), and is the mother church for the Diocese of York and the Province of York.

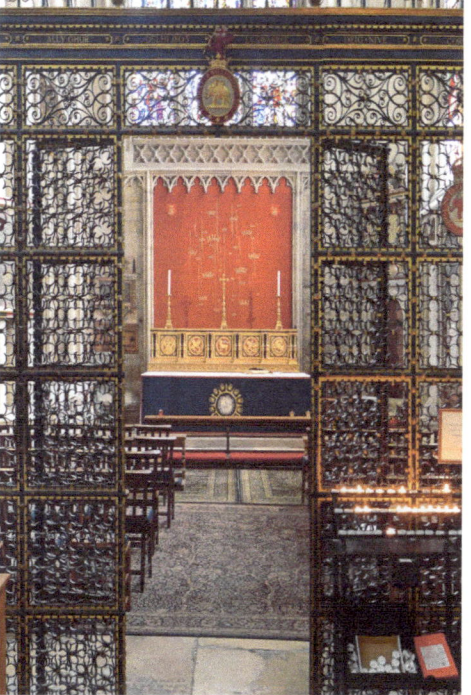

All Saints Chapel

St Peter

West face

Top of screen, St George's Chapel

GLOSSARY

Ambo : raised speaking stand

Apse : semicircular recess/extension

Aumbry : small cupboard/niche used to store sacred objects

Boss : ornamental covering of join of vaulting ribs

Capital : broader section of head of column

Cathedra : a bishop's official throne

Chancel : space reserved for clergy and choir

Chantry : endowment for priests to celebrate masses for soul of founder

Chapel : small worship space

Chapter House : building, usually round, where early monks read a daily chapter

Choir : space used by singing group (choir) and clergy

Clerestory : upper part of cathedral containing series of windows

Cloister : covered walk, typically with columns on one side around a quadrangle

Crossing : the intersection of nave and transepts

Font : receptacle for water used in baptism

Gothic : architectural style with characteristic pointed arches

Grisaille : monochrome painting, appearing in some windows

Icon : devotional painting on wood

Kneeler : cushion or bench for kneeling on

Lancet (window) : tall narrow window with pointed arch at top

Lantern : lamp; capped roof opening with glazed surround

Lectern : tall stand with sloping book rest on top

Misericord : supporting ledge on underside of hinged seat

Narthex : antechamber, large porch

Nave : rectangular space in cathedral where congregation sits

Norman : early architectural style with large columns and round arches

Pulpit : elevated platform used by preacher

Pulpitum : screen separating nave and choir

Quire : alternative spelling of choir; often used to denote choir seating

Reredos : ornamental screen behind the high altar

Romanesque : early architectural style with large columns and round arches

Rood : cross or crucifix high above entrance to chancel

Rose Window : circular window with tracery suggesting a rose

Sacristy : room where priest prepares for services

Sanctuary : most holy part of cathedral, usually East of chancel

Triforium : gallery or arcade above main arches and below clerestory

Vault : arched structure of masonry forming a ceiling or roof

Vestry : alternative word for sacristy

www.ingramcontent.com/pod-product-compliance
Lightning Source LLC
Chambersburg PA
CBHW050851010526
44107CB00047BA/1576